plenty-fish

Sarah James

plenty-fish

plenty-fish
Sarah James

ISBN: 978-0-9931201-2-1

First published July 2015 by:

Nine Arches Press
PO Box 6269
Rugby
CV21 9NL
United Kingdom

www.ninearchespress.com

Printed in Britain by:
The Russell Press Ltd.

Contents

La vie est une cerise	Life is a cherry
La mort est un noyau	Death is its stone
L'amour un cerisier.	Love a cherry tree

Jacques Prévert

— until everything
was rainbow, rainbow, rainbow!
And I let the fish go.

Elizabeth Bishop

Of fences

'Two roads diverged
in a yellow wood'
Robert Frost,
'The Road Not Taken'

'Our wills and fates
do so contrary run'
William Shakespeare,
Hamlet

Yes, two hands on the steering wheel
allow for manual precision,
or so the guides inform us.

Two sides allow a balanced debate,
or a complicated story.

Two attempts, a hope
of passing our failures.
Two failures, another proof
of past wrongs.

Two possibilities allow a choice, of dilemma.
In two minds allows that we are indeed human.

Two kidneys – a spare for selfless donation,
or half the work filtering mundane exchanges.

Two bulldozers won't mend fences.
Bulldog boundaries are not for sitting on.

Two hands cupped,
an arc for drinking;

two animals, arked,
did not allow for
the Woolly Mammoth,
Dodo, Steller's Sea Cow,
Falkland Islands Wolf,
Caribbean Monk Seal...

two elements,
say hydrogen and oxygen,
might allow
a molecular reaction.
Sometimes,
that makes water;
this vessel overflowing, maybe.

In two minds allows that we are human in deed.
Two hands joined, a more-than-flesh linking.

Two things which life does not allow:
words that can be throated back,
and bullets which re-enter a gun.

When Malala Yousafzai stepped
from the metal shell-shock
of her school bus, she raised
her book in both hands,
then softly spoke louder.

Journey of the Fruit

In the orangery, shrubs huddle,
hungry for rain and swelling
with citrus scents. Kumquats,
limes and an out-of-place yellow:
one green lemon tipping

towards plump exotic.
Zest curves snug in my palm,
a wholeness inhaled,
unlike the sliced moons of home's
shelved jar, leaching pale flecks.

And that star spreading down
from the fruit's goose-pimpled nipple.
Hint of hot safari sands,
cocktail cruises, the Charleston,
young Riviera sunshine unpeeled

miles away from home's
clouded glass, pith and split pips.
Far from centuries of shadows lined up
in curtsey to allowanced love
and orders of skin colour.

They hold out the damp trays
which circle each potted base, offer
Earl Grey with a sliver of fresh juice,
silver spoons glinting on porcelain,
beside thin cuts of lemon drizzle.

Not beyond now's memory, hands
still tremble.

Still the Apple

His mouth moon-craters my flesh,
curves tiny ribbons in flushed skin.
After gorging, he holds my skeleton
to the light, peers through small slits
between the ribs in search of a heart.
He does not find one, only the rust-
brown of the scalloped wounds left
by his teeth. Later, I'll bleed black.
For him, little change now, except
his lips' sometimes strained shape,
weighted down by past sweetness.

For Her, A Different Skin

Given the right blade, he might slit her.
Not for fox pelt sleekness, or rabbit warmth.

Hang legs from a rafter, limbs parted.
Not for the lush flush of raw pain.

Unseam a red circle; cut deeper.
Not for a bitter scream's squeezed juice.

Slice the underside, finger it from bone.
For the guts' intricacy untangled.

Slide away cartilage, loose from flesh.
For the pulsed butterflies, released.

Free intergluing membrane, slowly unsplice.
For the cracked almond heart, relieved.

Glide hand between, peel from carcass.
In hope of finding skin which fits,

without snicking any arteries.

Let's Remember

The therapist urges, then instructs me, to view
my life
as if from above, events pegged out on a line,
housewifely,
as though drying will smooth creases. But what if
memory's flaked,
its pastry rolled too thin; or clotted flour lumps,
then baked,
yeast-rise into tumours – thick clumps unbalancing
the whole?

We cannot force history, herd our recollections
from fields
into a farmyard pen to be fattened up for Christmas
family meals.

Yet, I see a child, palm mosaicked with blood
and broken
glass, green bottle fragments on a pantry floor.
Cold. I feel
a shawled baby patterned in cotton yellow
and cream,
cradled in my mother's strange young arms.
Her voice
is hushed sea in a shell, a whispered name's
sounds spliced
just like mine. But the shape of these echoes,
this child,
her baby, are not of me, then, or now. They are
my eye's

invention draped, pegless, across looking back's
faked twine.
Turned to ghosts since, and littered by the wind,
even as sunlight
hugs them into its shadows, this unstilled time.

Cutting to the Bone

i)

Those knives with pearled handles
stored up within velvet in my grandmother's drawer;
for her use only;
their tarnish handed down
with her tongue's sharp gifts.

Our daily ones: steel and something alloyed
against age's metal rainbows and the sweat of over-usage;
serrated, blunt;
sometimes coming together,
often clattering in cutlery harmonics;
cutlass-bent stabbing ice from the freezer.
Silences laid awkwardly beside them on the table.

The silvered set nested in black slits
until the urge for thin-filleting;
piercing thick skin;
wedging bread into neat slices of whiteness, crusts trimmed;
chopping layered onions to tears.

ii)

I've never doubted the fear
of what I might find if I braved myself,
and dug in a real blade.
So far only, perhaps,
before more than friction resists,
clogged with warm flesh,
and the outrage of armed nerves.
Bated gasp,
then from hole to gash in one forced red drowning.

From there, clamping back the ribs,
then, somehow, to those lungs,
vocalisation flattened now to pale plastic,
and below,
in that heart's cowed animalness
– their titanium points lodged –
so many years' words
quiver
with the deeper violence.

The *je ne sais quoi* of it

It's almost a kaleidoscoped dream: that year
lazing on the brasserie terrace, breathing after
his Gauloises, Pascal Obispo on the headphones.

But one word: say *oui*, a *non*, maybe a *peut-être*,
and I'm back in Prévert's *Déjeuner du Matin*,
replayed slowly in monochrome footage –

his lips on the rim of my white espresso cup;
his long fingers, stirring; the black
of his coated back, leaving; that silence afterwards –

which certain intonations still invoke now,
just as the *p, b, m* of his voice nuzzle
into my sleep, no matter how hard I try to keep

the hiss of fricatives memorised in my mouth.

I bite down on the memory

because images of merged bodies feed me;
　　because images of merged bodies in the wood
　　there where he killed himself are what he fed me;
　　　　because of that branch now hung on my back,
　　　　my back-to-front stomach filled with worms;
　　　　　　because of this heart of barbed wolf bone;
　　　　because I do, and suck the night without moon,
　　　　the shrivelled fruit berried without juice;
　　because my blood-blanched, arrow throat
　　can't swallow whole the taste of softness;
because I've forgotten how tongues may talk
and lips kiss, without the need to bite.

Elliptic

Alone, I watch the moon swell,
and ebb, its white hole cut

into a smooth page of spilled ink.
Cold night clots around this pale light.

A lunar footprint scratches just surface
dust but lasts for millions of years.

Unlike his fingerprint on that note;
final thoughts looped from black curves.

Viewed from here, our moon's sphere
is flatter than the world he left behind.

But look closer at its pitted crust:
shadows pass; orbits shift, if not for us.

From phases in the dark, lives lit by stars –
at least, that's what he whispered once.

I hold onto the words like a moonstone,
harden my fist around his imprint.

Walking under Water

Face uplifted, open to lightning,
my lone walk is startled
by the rain's sudden prattle

Leaves scramble dogwood;
mute green-veined tongues hide
blackbirds and loosed flowers

Clouds empty their cache:
a tip-tap, tap-tip binary
on thinly-clothed bones' tissue skin

I take in one drop on my tongue,
let my mouth close around
the choked oh! of absence

and listen to the rain sound
its relentless guttural
splattering

Cactus Ballgown

This dress should be kept for those prickly occasions
when you sense dryness, and wish to make a point.

Take care. Such sun-sanded satin is not easily
removed once you grow into its green sheen.

Do not plan on letting anyone close.
They will only get hurt. These flowers are not

for picking. Instead, strengthen your spine,
prepare for the pain of being justly deserted.

Above all, beware of the needles when you un-
dress alone, your skin riddled now with pins.

throughrose-tintedglasses/plentymore/
Drowningone'sclichés

my notepad and pen
(& metaphors of him)
drown in a half-glass of rosé

as I sip/slip, my hand's dissected;
edges leach until all I see
is ink-stained creases

I look at the pool below
– pale stretch of fake ocean –
everything swimming

no goodbyes to hold;
thoughts thrash
a distant meniscus

my fingers butterfly
through air; dive from the page –
my mind's wrecked lake

while I wait, I down time,
slake reflections
in another glass of wine

slurp back dreg-bubbles,
plenty-fish rising
from a shadowed sea floor

On the Brink of Adultery

(not at Dover Beach)

He says it's natural, that blinked-
back cliff-top urge to jump
and free-fall into dead space
as air rushes a vacuum.

Longing pulls us to sure gaps
between words, hands, lips –
to lunge. From firm ground
to forbidden sounds, fleshed.

Even before I'm wracked
by rocks' sharpened teeth,
the dive's shock rips deep.
Abrupted, sky spills.

Small Deceptions

i)

Not the rain that drips from clasped fingers,
magnifying their grained smallness.

Not the air that we breathe in, exhaling
later our own misted landscapes.

The blue, shaped mass of these things
held at distance – lakes, oceans, sky.

They masquerade for our eyes' delight
in silks of sapphire, iris, azure,

let hands and lungs explain transparency
and the thinness of our grasp.

ii)

If every colour is a different scattering of light,
a different blend of Hertz*

                              then even my hurt heart
is a sunset, shattering red, pink, peach.

iii)

A leopard that transforms its spots
without using paint, or photoshop.

iv)

Interlocking warm skin loosed
by slights of emphasis and tone:
from lust to last to lost

                          the list
of white lies laced in between
arcs of spectral light.

---

* *Specific frequencies of light reflected by an object trigger specific cones and rods in the eye. This determines which colours our brain perceives.*

This Holy Shrine

We are not pilgrims. Our feet ache, tempers
stumble in the Venetian heat. We seek
some shade in a street café, mouths struggling
with our own stubbed silence. Beneath the sign

Tera Farsetti, strangers' sandals push
shadows along the crazy paving, home
ground many thousand miles away from this
noon sun on lizard skin. Pouring water,

the clink of my bracelet's love heart on glass
breaks our glazed dumbness. *I miss the boys,*
he says. And there it is, our flesh union.
He rests one hand on mine. Its thin gold glints.

Wanting

It's his hands, always his hands.

How fingertips skip from the keyboard
to play arpeggios along my arm.

How the pressure of his palm
steadies the small of my back,
so warmth lingers.

How his index finger, which pushes down
on the knife chopping coriander for curry,
traces my thoughts, soothes creases
from letters, gives shape to my lips.

How that chunky 'c' of muscle and bone
curls around his pint glass lifting
from full to empty, full to empty,
while his other hand finger-taps
my beer mat till we synchronise rhythms.

How he pulls weeds from the mud,
hands clasped in a firm grasp
around stubborn necks,
or pushes a kiwi-fruit
from its hessian skin –
forceful, but persuasive.

How he snake-coil-palms
a plum stone sticky with juice,
once he's sucked the flesh clean;
that pincer-flick movement of air
propelling grapes to his tongue;
his thumb-finger grip on a sachet,
that quick pinch open...

how sometimes he uses his mouth.

Nomadic

I hiked miles to be here,
fingers tapping on this desk.
Dad's breath shrinks and expands
the room behind me.

I write down the cities I've lived in:
Winchester, Cardiff, Oxford, Rouen…
then, when I was brave enough to spin
the dust from his globe.

Returning now: its axle stilled;
my pen scratching blank paper;
the shushed 'here'
of polished wood on skin.

That click of his nails against teeth.
The glass-muted landscape of calves, pheasants and sheep.
Trying to sense my place in this,
I drown in the white noise –

mower stutters; a flown bird's silence;
higher, rustlings to and fro.

All the Flowers

i)

I place the anniversary bouquet
beside her name's curves.

The cemetery's spine has kinked,
its tarmac limbs spread.

Old trees cast new leaves
on Nan's stone, roots dug in.

I leave the overpowering scent
of lilies, lost in the wind.

ii)

After my dad arranges his own funeral
– the 'as and when' and 'just in case'

of his naked corpse
buried on the farmland within a day –

Mum places her Baked Alaska
onto their glass table with pride.

As we lick the last meringue sweetness
from our spoons, metal shines

brighter than white bones picked clean.

iii)

Later, in their garden with my camera,
I trap a bee on purple buddleia.

My focus hesitates between insect
and flower, falters…as I try to keep

all this vivid within the frame.
I remember then where fear started,

with loss falling around me.

Wired Flesh

The multi-socket on our lounge carpet
is a charged bomb of white plastic;
fuse-leads snaking.

My son rushes in, plants small explosions
of love on my cheeks, then settles
from kisses to LCD screen.

Computer in his lap, graphics trigger laughter,
frowns, sharp exclamations in code.
Aged eight, already part-strange to me.

Elsewhere, cornered, his big brother
plugged into the same game.
Speech disengages.

I pick up my machine, black weight
of electronics, and slot myself in.
Electricity ticks unheard, sparks ignite.

Mesmerised, false lives charm.
People pixelate around us.
Coiled somewhere in the wire tangle,

remnant arcs of bartered words,
that soft-flint of flesh fingers,
the fused touching of real skin.

Evolved

Pikathingy's winning! My son's hunched shoulders
unclench a smile as he looks up from his game
to high-five his brother. Then back down again.

Pikawotsit's an electric creature. This much
I've gleaned, I think. I've asked –
but Pikadespeak's faster than light-speed.

Least, it is to a Pikaignoramus. *They fight, right?*
– Yeah, but it's just fun, Mum, a contest,
like karate. None of them get hurt.

I try to engage with his *Pokémon*
as an interactive epic or modern fable.
But where's the moral to relate to?

I start to talk about Aesop's 'Wolf and the Kid'.
Huh, Mum? He glances up, then back.
I give up the goat, turn to the 'Tortoise and Hare'.

He doesn't even grunt. Clearly, I'm slow at evolving.
But I've learned from the Tortoise and Pikadeafness.
I unleash my voice's Raichu thunder.

** Raichu is a Pokémon game character that evolves from a less-powerful
creature when exposed to a Thunder Stone.*

Imprints

Absence is required at the school gate;
my kisses less than a wisp
of mist on the morning's
laughter-strung air.

His coated back is all I'm offered,
black fabric flying from a tear.
My dreams tied in stripes at his neck –
hopes caught...then loosed:

a robin tipped from cupped branches
to splash red – its feathers soft
against snow. Claws imprint
windowsill flowers.

These slight traces squeezed
from those bated-breath moments
when winds gust, skies darken
and gate hinges freeze closed.

Coffee Break

Purple-blue ribbons
diffuse in slow kite-tails
from a blackberry teabag.

Flutter-fingered, my son drops
an unopened sachet of sugar
into his cappuccino froth.

He asks me to pass a spoon:
a milk moustache on his lip,
his voice breaking.

Bagging Up

I found it this morning: a single pink bootee
gaping white like an empty shell.

When I see flowers,
or bonnets and frilly dresses
next to the boys' dungarees,
I picture you.

You should be grown tall by now.
But I can still hold you: fossilised
fragments from the scan cupped
in my hand; small as a bullet,

or hole in the heart.
I imagine dark curls and shy smile,
though when you speak,
it's merely an echo of their toddler talk.

I write this to you,
my child that never was,
yet is,
                    but

I write it for me –
though words won't bend
to explain that longing for you,
I love the boys no less.

So, as I fold away bibs and bodysuits
and bag up blue for my friends,
the pink of your bootee creases my thoughts.
I ought to throw it, finish this, say goodbye...

Instead, I reach up, hide it high
in a cupboard my sons must never find.

Against the Vacuum

Leaves sway the sunlight, illuminate dust
on the dashboard. Flecks of skin: his, mine,
our children's. Dead cells mingle in the vents.

Specks bounce from the speakers –
slight, almost insignificant, they cling
to the air, the plastic, its surrounding fibres.

We leave the shape of our handprints
dark in their cloistered whiteness,
let discarded lives travel with us.

And When

Blue lights sequence incessantly –
LED-blips strung at life's corners,

while the tumble dryer grinds on daily;
clothes slap metal, settle, slap.

Water drains thin. Skies of strained
ocean blanch at their own wideness

broken only by the script
of bird flight and stripped branches.

My neoned retina stitched from strange
fragments of nucleus, unstranded.

Inheritances bicker. The right hip screams,
 "Cripple!" My left, "Hurry up."

Without glass, my eyes sense little.
My pancreas is less than a withered

leaf on its beaten-up stalk.
To each their own abstractions

in tissue, these encoded failings,
while air bleaches, days thin, metal

turns, lights flash. Years lake.
Fears rise from tinnitus to siren –

no swerving from the neon blip
that now crushes towards me.

Home

The shapes and sounds of it defeat me.
There is a lake, or sea,
though the water may be light,
or music, or shadows
falling from the air's tightrope.

Once, it was a pebbled hand
curled inside another's.
There were skimmed stones then,
and white butterflies on lavender.
Roots deep, but unseen.

Now? Silhouettes flit
across cracked walls.
No place for a doorbell.
What is not within the hand's control
falls as the laws of physics govern.

I should die first –
the recent past disturbs;
my childhood laughter
is dislodged from old gables.
Unsettled dust layers my wet face.

Everything metal, now with sea crust.
I wipe away spilt brine,
then build myself an ark from his rafters.
I season the keel with thick lavender
to brave the salt sting.

Losing Faith

Take home a whole shoal from the fair.
Name them Matthew, Mark, maybe John.

Watch how their varnished orange peel
teases through the bubble's knotted plastic.

Give them a bigger tank to swim in:
a glassed reality of gravel and weeds.

The hide and seek begins. That curving
around stones. The flitting outline of soft bones.

That deceptive width of tails almost thinned
to water's transparency. Thick smears

on surfaces tinged green by sunlight's
revelations. Soon their names flake.

After death, you flush away each, past
twitching. Your son demands a prayer.

Past Sacrificial

The fishmonger scoops sprats
from their ice bed, bags them.
Back home, I knife open
the plastic. Shock.
Bladderwrack knots lungs.

Nausea settled, I unroll
my stilled daggers.
Textured silver traps light.
Twelve eyes of flattened metal,
hole-punched with night.

And the blood. Not stale juice
in dried mud rivulets.
A rose-pink spill, petalling
the gills and mouths of lithe bodies
otherwise past rainbow hooks.

Though their scales change
shade with my movements,
their fins are dead leaves'
pinned vein traces.
Only the tails left alive –

even now, they tease me
with sea-blue promises,
all the while still flaunting
the slipperiness of life,
and death's strong stench.

Transplanted

The gardeners sow the seeds
into rows of furrowed flesh,
stripped to protein skeletons

Stem cells multiply, colonise, grow

From these 'ghost' chambers
hollowed into pig and rat hearts,
a strange hope beats

Wonders multiply, colonise, grow

In this orchard, stripped bare
of apples, branches bend
with pulsating flesh

Windfalls cruelly multiply

Some Prayer

Toadstools cluster,
pale shivers of cold sun.
Nearer, each a jutting nail
softened to throbbing nipple.
Beige flesh tacked down, pert
between grass clumps, shuffles
attention, out and in. That rush
as wind harries autumn leaves.
Forget gravity, forget north –
this force is in all directions.
Its hurried thrusts of air lift
nature's time-eaten edges,
brush atoms across bark
and bare skin in a flurry
of constant osmosis.

Meditation on/with/for a Buzz

That winter I hang with the bees
above hibernation and frost.

Eyes, ears, nose are nectar-
combs my mind slices for honey.

From candled sense babble – wings
of tree blossom, cinnamon,

crossed legs & slanted
stalked-apple berets – a stillness:

the everyday arbitrary,
apple-stalk-picked.

White

It clutches ghosts while we sleep,
brittles grass, fragments paths,
corpses leaves. My feet crack
across its uncertainty: this fractured

daze as to what world I wake in.
Again, yet different. Changed,
yet still the same. Life crouches
low in its cold throat, rasping.

In the park, oaks resist enforced
patterns, retain their bark scales.
My trainers scrape at the whiteness,
refuse to accept this frost's rigidity.

For a minute, light lifts,
then melts back to black fabric.

Re. Composition

The sun is perfect. My orange poppy glows.
I position myself and my tripod; poised
to take a prize-winning picture.
Then, I see it staining
a rain-washed petal
like the mark from a dirty hat pin.
I reach forward to brush it away – and stop.
Light shifts. I see a French knot,
legs unpicking silk stitches,
rainbows bending across its back.
I glimpse something ungraspable –
every bit black, every bit beautiful,
every bit perfect
ant.

In the Ointment

Always a fly: Koko juggles
one bigger than his hand
in his en pirouette
cartoon clown dance;

the blot in *Brazil's* ministries
of info/records/retrieval –
from Tuttle to Buttle
in one deadly misfax.

Lording it! Swarming it!
Hoarding up bluebottled trouble,
– the stirring unrest
of air, fingers and germs,

revolting. Always a fly,
the smallest of things,
this full stop with wings
that keeps moving

the goalposts; as if
to get a buzz from it!

Notes in the ointment: Max Fleischer and his silent cartoon
character Koko the Clown are bothered by a fly in *The
Tantalizing Fly*, 1919. Terry Gilliam's 1985 dark comedic
fantasy film *Brazil* opens with a swatted fly causing a
misprint which has fatal consequences. Also, William
Golding's dystopian novel *Lord of the Flies*, 1954.

His Wife

The psychologist stares; tick.
As if eyes are glass openings,
and he's trying to lift the catch;

click. To get fully inside, he prises
the clock-case door, examines
cogs, levers, pulleys – tock –

the hammers for chiming. Now
sticking. A scrapyard of brass bits
around the brain's pendulum!

This slick exclamation stopped.
His pliers unpick, remove each blocked
piece which time has worked loose.

He checks the moon-phase, replaces
shock absorbers, re-sets
the balance wheel and escapement.

Next, polish, oil, coils realigned;
fixing nicked wires; tightening.
He bends closer, his eyes dulled

to shadow-bevelled sockets.
Behind his glass gaze,
bared metal ticks.

Shells

i)

Low tide: she digs a trench,
fills the children's bucket,
upturns its curved neatness.

And again, as many times as they ask,
fingers rushing to help her.
Edges crumble, give way to the sky.

Still, one son stakes a razor shell.
The other adds a stick flag.
Their Dad takes a picture.

ii)

Now he is hunched emptiness,
face buried in their bed.

Those hands, which fashioned
air, snow and sand into angels,
have calcified to closed fists.

Her pain has scoured him thin,
worn strength to luminescence.

Spilled sea drenches their duvet.

iii)

She pulls away from the thing
which has invaded her body.

It scuttles inside, pushes at bones.

When she opens her palm,
nothing to hold onto.

Her fingers clench crab-claw tight.

iv)

Water replaces her skin. | She no longer feels rain
on her face | or the waves at her feet. | The sea's
echoes | swill her hollow shape.

Van Gogh's Other Mistress

When she smells their daughter's citrus scent,
oranges fill her mouth and throat,
sweet from Arles.

When their son's hair strokes her cheek,
she savours ice-cream melting, vanilla
sunflowers on her tongue.

When his whisper brushes old promises,
she hears his ear unspiral;
her teeth crunch on bone.

She tastes nothing but paint.

Pied

A mostly unsilvered disco globe
hangs with five unlit bulb planets
in the squat's cracked window.

A shadow jigs: an arrhythmic
jolting, though it may be him
manoeuvring the flute for her.

Night digs at the sun, buries its dirt
in her nails. The music's bruise turns
from forced blue to smudged brown.

Even the street light's star sheds
its skin. Shreds catch on the bare
tree's teeth. He tells her to watch

the planets drown like rats
trapped in his liquid black glass.
Silence presses hard at her lips.

through glass

i)

The lead-edged light of childhood memories.
Stubbed-toe sandals and fly-away dresses.
Laughter freeze-framed and albumed.

Her Gramp's false eye, Nan's specs,
Dad's smashed-bottle tone,
her Mum's molten-blown heart –

the trapped bubbles within.

ii)

From conception, the empty vase of her,
into which transparency's poured;
DNA strands twisted into stalks.

That changeling inside her,
its stained-glass feathers clinking
against her skeleton. The sharp twinge

of brittle bone, cracked.

iii)

The crystal hummingbird hanging
part-rainbows on their kitchen floor:
a broken-beak present from her son,
singing the silence of absence.

iv)

High up, the chapel's petalled windows.
Across the tiles, patterned leaf haloes:
a glimpse of trees beyond this cold stone,
where the sun's shadow brood plays ghosts.

v)

She lies corpse-still in a petri dish,
lets the therapist prod her
with questions she cannot answer.

Her mind pressed flat
between slide and cover slip,
his microscope eye
is black, white and brown staring down.

She tells him she doesn't know
the shape of her other glass life,
but fears the best has passed her by.

vi)

Steam condenses to hieroglyphics
on the shower screen and mirror,
where even her thin breath

leaves a passing mark,

though her mouth is husked
behind the mist of its slightness.

vii)

Courgettes polytunnelled,
strawberries redden in the greenhouse;
her rain barrel nozzle, hosepipe unsnaked,
water directed and flowing –

its liquid glass
transforms her hands
into solid tools
divining and growing.

Museum Offering

Neuropteris hollandica
Upper Carboniferous, Westphalian B, Duckmantian Stage

This fossil alters the shape of my palm.
Flesh moulds to its mineral coldness,
as its mitten leaves offer up past lives
dislodged from a Wigan roof shale.

Dead Latin filters through exhibits.
Fern veins thread through cracked stone,
imprint history as mine shafts have outlined
our landscape: pitted surfaces, that sense

of old ground shifting. No sign of the hands
which worked those sulphured coal seams.
This fern's known the weight of growth
and darkness, how fragility hardens.

Soft cells reduced to skeleton strength,
its shape is still cast into rock millions
of shades of sunlight later. Movement
continues around it: hands touch, feet pace,

voices fill our fields, parks, streets…
I place this firm ground in my pocket.

The Hummingbird Case

Delicate beaks poised,
elegant light-strumming wings
pinned unhumming
to a broken twig frame.

A filigree of holes, this lacework
tree of feather and claw.
Distanced, death's plumage
not so brittle, so torn.

This case shimmers with lives
spun from sun, textured
with oceans, forests, skies...
What's done is done. Yet,

even as I reach for the gleam
of these half-kiss scissor tails,
I feel silence cut.
To seize the beaks, tug them and...

my stillness snaps their wings.

Bewitching
Halloween at Muncaster

We sleep in the castle's crucifix lodge.
Roped garlic hangs from the wardrobe,
the bearded roots dribble clumped mud,
almost dried blood. Strange vapours
mist the windows. Ink cap mushrooms
lie sliced to thin ghosts on the sill.

The porch collects birch twigs, cats
and a spellbinding past, where country life
was conjured up as witchcraft. Unlike
the giant stride of our electric men,
their wired arms flying heat and light
into these cold, dark landscapes.

All sparks of mystery firmly earthed.
In place of old ways, everything tested,
proved, explained. Except how stars
speed away from us faster than gravity
should allow, while the lit-up castle
projects its own constellations

to wow the night sky – magic still cast,
and drowned, in the beholder's eye.

* *Currently, the universe's rate of expansion is accelerating when laws of gravity should mean it is decelerating.*

Looking Back *In Fragments*

Summer still won't come.[1]

It's always the winter lake,[2]   *with a free-fall*
of orange dusk –   *that thrusts*
deep trees in deeper.   *Their leaves jump after.*

Wind clenches fingers,   *pulls you closer...*
if you don't break   *this memory*
freeze-framed in that now...[3]

But his place has shaped itself   *to your bones,*[4]
                    taken home your name
as hard ice in its mouth.[5]

The echo of his whispers[6]   *fills your mind with snow;*
a blizzard of thoughts   *swirled*
to red-edged numbness.[7]

No summer thaws here.[8]

----

not(e) a poetics of glass/water

[1.] Objective art was not reality, | just one undiluted version of it |
That was her belief. | There were other taut thoughts. | Like her
relationships, | not all of them held water.

[2.] At the heart of water's pulse, | repetition. Its rhythms against
stone. | And everything's return: river | to sea, to cloud, to rain,
to stream, | to river. A fluid language; | the bound sounds within,

| a sometimes silver habit, | other times muddy. Recognition | flowing from repetition. | Repetition slowing change, | change frozen by this braking. | Liquid motion now a solid | chain of invisible links; | fixed in less-glistening. | The logic of reaching | emotional understanding | through the fact of repeating | is only partly mirrored in her life.

3. That winter, water refused to flow. | The river froze; turned to cold glass. | Her landscape metamorphosed; | veins became snow.

4. As if through water or glass darkly. | Here, the very acts of habit | form their unbreaking; | those grounded in sense | and those formed unsoundly.

5. clar·it·y n. 1. through glass starkly | 2. the most deceptive of illusions | 3. whereby elision may become allusion.

6. As water trickles through rock.

7. The language of suffering still linked them, | as if written into their blood | by the evil genius of forsaken gods. | Neither their words nor that pain | could be watered down.

8. These fragments were later rescued | from the ashes and burnt timbers | of the ferryman's boathouse. | It is believed the coldness | of the stone foundations | protected them from the fire, | along with a danake, | the broken links of iron chains | and some unidentified | human bones. | The rest of the manuscript | was never found and | the ferryman himself | was presumed drowned.

The Philosopher's Magnum Opus

Strangely, no real effort is required,
only time, and the sea's tidal wisdom.

Lodged in scalloped soft tissue,
concentric layers thicken

over past irritations. These pearls
are the stones which cannot be faked.

No. Smoothed from ridged enamel,
grained with our tongues' textures,

each offering soundly strung: "My love,"
"What do you need?" "Let me help you."

Set them now, glistening without wetness,
among the sharp rocks and black shingle.

Raindrop on a Red Leaf

His hand cupping a spider, wrist trembling;
a thin branch in the wind,

or the lurch of lungs and stomach when a plane
takes off and the world sinks away,

or the first bead of bone clearly conceived
from that scan's black smudge.

Suspension of time itself, the moment's
gasp of skin and lips,

when the whole future balances
on the wet leaves of two tongues.

Too Modest

after Lorine Niedecker

Lone 'plover':
        contents shaped
     from marsh mud & Rock banks

That anon can
        thru which cut
    lines shine

A rhythm river trimmed
        with reeds,
    silver fish & light slivers

From Grasmere

i)

the morning sky peers
through rustle leaves and shadow
glimpses of blue eyes

Ink on white paper. His pen
links. Letters flow in rivers.

a lone magpie pecks
for life buried below ground
worms in frost sparkle

His words sturdy oaks, set out
in neat rows even when felled.

ragged slant of grass
Her rough note slack next to his?

ii)

Domestic whispers. Journalled
away, hushed in his presence.

> *ladybirds idle*
> *spiders catch flies in the dust*
> *blown petals scatter*

Curtains drawn across darkness.
Linen pressed into firm lines.

> *fisticuff birdsong*
> *cold creeps through cracks, rattles doors*
> *ice hardens edges*

Her right place with him, in time –
> *high risk of a storm*

Against Candlelight

As marbled wax melts, flickers
of unknown lives beckon
from fire's hypnotic chaining.

Colliers, chandlers and cavemen
gaze with me: my desk a shock
of print-outs, letters and confusions.

I try to rope these family scraps
together, to secure
the past on which I exist,

but the string I have twisted
to makeshift wick
coils downwards, limply.

A bread-thief stoned to death,
the wyuen pine of a ducking-stool,
Saxon kings' golden burial mounds…

Bones beneath the ground;
memory in black smoke.
I feed the paper skeleton

of my great-great-grandmother's unwed pain
to the wick's relentless flame,
then pinch out its burn.

Snatches of the Rivers and Moor

In stubbled grass, stags arch.
Sparked clouds held high, patches
of sky hang from their antlers.

> *here now, here then, a hand meets*
> *a hand, and curves to frame it*

A brush of dark trees. Blue daubs
blanched winter borders.
Snow rubs the moor's feet.

> *the tracks of once footprints*
> *follow, dissect, intermingle*

Anchored, ships in the harbour await
tide-time's holler. Beguiled, they slip loose,
sift to and from shore greenness.

> *this sound fluted into our bones*
> *knows the edge of heathered silence*

Into the mist that is sunlight and slopes;
the landscape elopes, then re-emerges,
outline firmed by its shadows.

> *stand back from your tautest cliff,*
> *lift from the rivers, pause* with the curlew*

* *The curlew sign was created by Benjamin Britten for his church parable* Curlew River *(1964), which has no conductor. This pause mark is placed above a note or rest to allow musicians or singers to come back into synchronisation.*

Endurance

Stubborn roots draw up strength
from the land's glacial inheritance,

set the stem's *Taraxacum* slant, push
its head through drought and brambles,

steady its unbalanced mass against winds
and raindrops' Cossack dances.

Our father's father in the garden.
His calloused hands – thorns

embedded in weathered skin –
beating back weeds with his stick.

Each blow determines those angles
of stony resistance,

despite a leadened stoop
and the nearing of last rites.

When time comes, we nudge
ashen parachutes into short flight.

Asterisks fall at our feet;
find cracks in the hard earth

to grow from: defiant stars on stilts,
striking up at the sky.

Taraxacum officinale is the scientific name for the common dandelion.

Oil and Water

'HURRY UP PLEASE ITS TIME'
T.S. Eliot, 'The Waste Land'

The Fisher King's archaeology of earth and sky,
his wide eye glazed by time's distance:

          cirrus
    cumulo   nimbus   alto   stratus
blue green honeyed green brown green honey tan blue

From above, instead of cross-section: the coastline;
a broken enamel plate of ochre dark-solder-hedges
honey green walls-running-in-between gold rust.

Note the Ice Age lie of the land,
the blunted stones of the Grange circle,
lives layered into fields, cut to…

the rain that stings the world's faces.
Air thickening here to a dense dust breathing.
There, a gulp, a splutter, a half-gagged half-

They say that they tortured them by pouring
water over their mouths in one continuous
near-drowning. Not their fault, of course. They

made this out
rage inevitable.
Elsewhere,

the bore-holes of the mantle's stigmata,
tar blackening the fished seas' white wings,
the acid feathers of moulting stone.

Even in America.
Beverly McGuire turns on a tap: nothing.
The view from her back porch: nine oil wells,

fracking trucks and drills, dry ranch land
abandoned, cotton fields emptied of crops,
Texan tempers crack.

Their grease lacquers separating
us from settling the shape of history?
Or our letting the future

break into shale flakes,
each carbon hour tagged and dated
in terabytes, dollar signs and tanks?

The black spot is on our hands.

Acknowledgements

Acknowledgements are due to the editors, curators and organisers of the following publications, webzines, exhibitions, projects and competitions, where versions of some of these poems originally appeared:

'Of fences' in *Here Comes Everyone*; 'Journey of the Fruit' on the National Trust's Hanbury Hall website; 'Still the Apple' in *Envoi*; 'For Her, A Different Skin' in *Hallelujah for 50ft Women* (Bloodaxe); 'Let's Remember' and 'throughrose-tintedglasses/plentymore/ Drowningone'sclichés' on *Kumquat Poetry*; 'The *je ne sais quoi* of it' in *Britmag*; 'I bite down on the memory' in *The Rialto*; 'Elliptic' and 'Shells' (renamed) shortlisted in the Ilkley Literary Festival Poetry Competition 2012; 'Cactus Ballgown', 'Re. Composition' and 'The Hummingbird Case' in *Magma*; 'Wanting' in The Poetry School brochure; 'Evolved' in *Poetry News*; 'Coffee Break' and 'Against the Vacuum' on *Nutshells and Nuggets*; 'Bagging Up' on *The Guardian* online; 'And When' in *Abridged*; 'Transplanted' winner in the Oxford University / Radcliffe Science Library Parallel Universe poetry competition 2013, exhibited in the Radcliffe Science Library, the History of Science Museum and on the Bodleian Library website; 'Meditation on/with/ for a Buzz' in *Tears in the Fence*; 'His Wife' and 'Shells' in *Obsessed With Pipework*; 'In the Ointment' in *Verse Kraken*; 'Van Gogh's Other Mistress' in *A Complicated Way of Being Ignored: The Grist anthology of the best poetry of 2012*; 'Pied' in *Under the Radar*; 'Museum Offering' in the North West Poets anthology *Sculpted*; 'The

Philosopher's Magnum Opus' in the *Drifting Down the Lane* anthology; 'Raindrop on a Red Leaf' on *Tuck* journal and Worcestershire buses, as part of a Worcestershire Arts Partnership/CBS Outdoors/First Capital Connect commission; 'Snatches of the Rivers and Moor' second prize in the Hope Bourne Poetry Competition 2012, and published in the *Exmoor Review*; 'Endurance' in *The Lake*; 'Oil and Water' in *The Wolf*.

Background facts for 'Oil and Water' from *The Guardian* article 'A Texan tragedy: ample oil, no water' by Suzanne Goldenberg.

Further thanks to Manchester Writing School fellow MA poetry students and staff, particularly my workshop and portfolio supervisors Michael Symmons Roberts, Adam O'Riordan and Jean Sprackland; Alec Newman and Jane Commane for editorial advice; the Writing West Midlands Room 204 scheme; Worcestershire Poetry Society Stanza, particularly John Lawrence and Kathy Gee; poetry collaborators and friends Ruth Stacey, Ann Reed and Dan Haynes; and Justin Leavesley.